THIS JOURNAL
BELONGS TO

....

CLARKSON POTTER/PUBLISHERS
NEW YORK

Words matter, for
Language is an ark.
Yes,
Language is an art,
An articulate artifact.
Language is a life craft.
Yes,
Language is a life raft.

....

FROM "WHAT WE CARRY"

LIFE

....

Life is not what is promised,
But what is sought.
These bones, not what is found,
But what we've fought.
Our truth, not what we said,
But what we thought.
Our lesson, all we have taken
& all we have brought.

& what exactly are we supposed to be doing?

Penning a letter to the world.

FROM "SHIP'S MANIFEST"

You will be told now is not the time
For change to begin,
Told that we cannot win.
But the point of protest isn't winning;
It's holding fast to the promise of freedom,
Even when fast victory is not promised.

....

FROM "FURY & FAITH"

The future isn't attained.
It is atoned, until
It is at one with history,
Until home is more than a memory,
Until we can hold near
Who we hold dear.

....

FROM "CORDAGE, OR ATONEMENT"

We are walking beside our ancestors,
Their drums roar for us,
Their feet stomp at our life.
There is power in being robbed
& still choosing to dance.

....

FROM "SCHOOL'S OUT"

We might not be fully sure of all that we are.

& yet we have endured all that we were.

FROM "SURVIVING"

We are

       Arborescent—

What goes

       Unseen

Is at the very

       Root of ourselves.

....

FROM "ARBORESCENT I"

Storytelling is the way that unarticulated memory becomes art, becomes artifact, becomes fact, becomes felt again, becomes free.

FROM "PRE-MEMORY"

That's what only words can do—
Prod us toward something new
& in doing so, move us closer → together

. . . .

FROM "ANOTHER NAUTICAL"

What we have lived
Remains indecipherable.
& yet we remain.
& still, we write.
& so, we write.
Watch us move above the fog
Like a promontory at dusk.
Shall this leave us bitter?
      Or better?

....

FROM "THE SHALLOWS"

We do not hope for no reason.

Hope is the reason for itself.

FROM "ARBORESCENT III, or ELPIS"

Hope is the soft bird
We send across the sea
To see if this earth is still home.

....

FROM "ANOTHER NAUTICAL"

Hope is no silent harbor, no haven still.

It is the roaring thing that tugs us away

From the very shores we clutch.

FROM "LIGHTHOUSE"

Since the world is round,
There is no way to walk away
From each other, for even then
We are coming back together.

....

FROM "& SO"

Our mask is no veil, but a view.

What are we, if not what we see in another.

FROM "THERE'S NO POWER LIKE HOME"

We ignite not in the light, but in lack thereof,
For it is in loss that we truly learn to love.
In this chaos, we will discover clarity.
In suffering, we must find solidarity.

....

FROM "THE MIRACLE OF MORNING"

Who are we, if not

What we make of the dark.

FROM "THE UNORDINARY WORLD"

Though we have never met,
We have sensed the other all along,
Quiet & wandering, wide-lit
With the urge to move forward.
No human is a stranger to us.

....

FROM "LIGHTHOUSE"

And so we lift our gazes not
To what stands between us,
But what stands before us.
We close the divide,
Because we know to put
Our future first, we must first
Put our differences aside.
We lay down our arms
So that we can reach our arms out to one another.

....

FROM "THE HILL WE CLIMB"

When day comes, we step out of the shade,
Aflame and unafraid.
The new dawn blooms as we free it,
For there is always light,
If only we're brave enough to see it,
If only we're brave enough to be it.

....

FROM "THE HILL WE CLIMB"

What we carry means we survive,

It is what survives us.

We have survived us.

FROM "GOOD GRIEF"

Our scars are the brightest
Parts of us.

....

FROM "LUCENT"

To love is to be liable

To ourselves & each other.

FROM "CAPTIVE"

If we are to summon
Anyone or anything,
Let it be our tender selves.

....

FROM "WHO WE GONNA CALL"

Like a page, we are only legible

When opened to one another.

FROM "COMPASS"

We wonder how close
Can we come to light
Before we shut our eyes.
How long can we stand the dark
Before we become more than our shadows.

....

FROM "HEPHAESTUS"

Lost as we feel, there is no better
Compass than compassion.
We find ourselves not by being
The most seen, but the most seeing.

....

FROM "COMPASS"

The hardest part of grief

Is giving it a name.

FROM "COMPASS"

Scripture tells us to envision that:
"Everyone shall sit under their own vine and fig tree,
And no one shall make them afraid."
If we're to live up to our own time, then victory
Won't lie in the blade, but in all the bridges we've made.
That is the promised glade,
The hill we climb, if only we dare it:
Because being American is more than a pride we inherit—
It's the past we step into and how we repair it.

....

FROM "THE HILL WE CLIMB"

EVERY DAY WE ARE LEARNING

....

Every day we are learning
How to live with essence, not ease.
How to move with haste, never hate.
How to leave this pain that is beyond us
Behind us.
Just like a skill or any art,
We cannot possess hope without practicing it.
It is the most fundamental craft we demand of ourselves.

The earth is a magic act;

Each second something beautiful

On its stage vanishes,

As if merely going home.

FROM "IN THE DEEP"

What are we doing?
            Listening.
It took us losing ourselves
To see we require no kingdom
But this kinship.
It is the nightmare, never
The dream, that shocks us awake.

....

FROM "IN THE DEEP"

Anxiety is a living body,
Poised beside us like a shadow.
It is the last creature standing,
The only beast who loves us
Enough to stay.

....

FROM "FUGUE"

Strength is separate from survival.

What endures isn't always what escapes

& what is withered can still withstand.

FROM "CORDAGE, OR ATONEMENT"

Our need for nature
Is our need for origins,
The green tangled place
Where we are of least consequence
& yet still matter as much as anything.

....

FROM "CAPTIVE"

In this truth, in this faith, we trust.

For while we have our eyes on the future,

History has its eyes on us.

FROM "THE HILL WE CLIMB"

All we know so far is we are so far
From what we know.

....

FROM "PRE-MEMORY"

In this one life, we, like our joy, are fleeting but certain,

abstract & absolute, ghosts who glow & glow.

FROM "WHEN"

It's said that
ignorance is bliss.
Ignorance is this:
a vine that sneaks
up a tree, killing not
by poison, but by

blocking out
its light. . . .
Ignorance isn't bliss.
Ignorance is to miss:
to block ourselves
from seeing sky.

FROM "*VALE* OF THE SHADOW OF DEATH OR
EXTRA! EXTRA! READ ALL ABOUT IT!"

We're still willing to believe

Peace is a place on earth.

FROM "WAR: WHAT, IS IT GOOD?"

Anyone who has lived
Is an historian & an artifact,
For they hold all their time within them.

....

FROM "_ _ _ _ _ [GATED]"

In Spanish,
the word for
value is the
same as for
bravery: valor.

Courage must cost us something, or else it is worth nothing at all.

FROM *"VALE* OF THE SHADOW OF DEATH OR
EXTRA! EXTRA! READ ALL ABOUT IT!"

So when you're told that your rage is reactionary,

Remind yourself that rage is our right.

It teaches us it is time to fight.

FROM "FURY & FAITH"

Black lives matter,
No matter what.
Black lives are worth living,
Worth defending,
Worth every struggle.
We owe it to the fallen to fight,
But we owe it to ourselves to never stay kneeling
When the day calls us to stand.

....

FROM "FURY & FAITH"

We stand still,

If just to insist

That we still

Exist.

FROM "THE TRUTH IN ONE NATION"

Some days we believe
In nothing
But belief. But
It is enough to carry us forward.

....

FROM "THE TRUTH IN ONE NATION"

While we might feel small, separate & all alone,

Our people have never been more closely tethered.

The question isn't *if* we can weather this unknown,

But *how* we will weather this unknown together.

FROM "THE MIRACLE OF MORNING"

The only way to correctly predict
The future is to pave it,
        Is to brave it.
The breakage is where we begin.
The rupture is for remembering.

....

FROM "AUGURY OR THE BIRDS"

To love just may be

The fight of our lives.

FROM "WAR: WHAT, IS IT GOOD?"

Whether we prevail is not determined
By all the challenges that are present,
But by all the change that is possible.

....

FROM "FURY & FAITH"

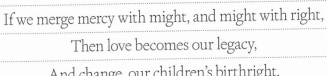

If we merge mercy with might, and might with right,
Then love becomes our legacy,
And change, our children's birthright.

FROM "THE HILL WE CLIMB"

Together, we envision a land that is liberated, not lawless.

We create a future that is free, not flawless.

Again & again, over & over,

We will stride up every mountainside,

Magnanimous & modest.

We will be protected & served

By a force that is honored & honest.

This is more than protest.

It's a promise.

....

FROM "FURY & FAITH"

The text this work is taken from:
The Hill We Climb (New York: Viking Books, 2021)
and *Call Us What We Carry* (New York: Viking Books, 2021).

ISBN 978-0-593-79689-4

Printed in Malaysia

Illustrations by Emma Shoshanna Shaw

Editors: Sara Neville and Sahara Clement
Designer: Lise Sukhu
Art director: Danielle Deschenes
Production editor: Joyce Wong
Production manager: Kelli Tokos

10 9 8 7 6 5 4 3 2 1

First Edition